The Art of Play

Contents

(Above) Woods of Net, p.122.
(Right) The Rampart Wave, p.268.

Sure, swings and roundabouts are fun...

But what about shooting from the maws of a grotesque, three-tongued monster, or traversing the body of a sleeping giant, scrabbling up his snaking cravat before whizzing down his coat tails? Why waste your time with seesaws and spinners when you can vault through a Victorian slate mine on colossal bouncy nets or scale a celebrated artist's monumental sculpture, the likes of which are typically reserved for admiring – and definitely not touching.

Faced with the choice between standard playground equipment and more innovative environments devised to foster open-ended play, my kids (and every other child I know) will invariably gravitate towards the latter. Visits to our local park largely result in them abandoning the standard-issue 1990s climbing frame in favour of the adjacent 60-tonne granite boulder, installed there several years later, which becomes a mountain, an island, a planet.

In a world full of rules, such non-prescriptive playgrounds feel deliciously liberating, granting kids the space to act wholly on impulse. Just as a great work of art compels us to empathise, feel and learn, a truly great playground wields the power to accelerate children's development, hone their problem-solving skills and encourage collaboration, all while inspiring boundless creativity (as opposed to simply getting them out of the house when they're being a bit rowdy).

In reality, play and art have a lot more in common than we might think. This book is a celebration of what happens when the two worlds collide. A salute to the artists, architects and playground designers who think outside the (sand)box, ushering the artistic realm in through the playground gate. More than that, it's the conciliation of two disciplines that, ultimately, derive from the same root – that of humanity's endless creativity. Playground designers must respond to inestimable social issues, from non-inclusion to deprivation and community decline, all while endeavouring to create something aesthetically pleasing.

Indeed, knockout modern playscapes like those dreamt up by Danish designer Monstrum are putting more traditional schemes to shame, swapping conical climbers and helter-skelters for towering zombie robots with slides for arms (p.250), fire-breathing dragons primed for medieval adventures (p.194) and playgrounds themed around everything from sea lions to samovars. Far beyond the confines of a traditional play area's remit, these inventive spaces grant kids the freedom to scale walls, explore hidden realms and play diverse roles within the playground universe.

Egon Møller-Nielsen's 'Tufsen' play sculpture, Stockholm, 1949.

And it's not just in Europe. Local governments across the globe are beginning to recognise the value of inventive design, and commissioning ever more fantastical playgrounds. In China, the popularity of playscapes such as Xisui Design's ambitious landscaped, Mars-inspired space (p.258) and studio X+Living's patterned pastel dreamscape (p.260) suggest an appetite for highly escapist concepts, while in Australia the success of Mike Hewson's Rocks on Wheels (p.36) points to a desire for riskier, more humorous playgrounds. Better still, many are building solutions that satisfy everyone, combining exciting spaces for childs' play, safe teen hangouts and appealing meeting places for adults, all while enhancing the wider urban landscape. Take, for example, 100architects' Pixeland (p.134), whose modular form allows for play, exercise and socialising; or the KuKuk Box in Phorms Schoolyard (p.219), which accommodates different age groups through multi-storey spaces for climbing, playing and hanging out. But such contemporary structures, while refreshing, are really nothing new.

In 1949, Danish sculptor Egon Møller-Nielsen installed his abstract 'Tufsen' play sculpture in a park in Stockholm. Cast from a mix of crushed concrete and marble, this otherworldly, Swiss-cheese-like blob satisfied children's desire to hide, slide, climb and enjoy a taste of danger – all while looking a million miles from any playground they'd seen before. The first of its kind, Tufsen marked a significant shift in playground design, as the once sharply defined boundaries between play, art and public space began to blur. Around the same time in Amsterdam, architect Aldo van Eyck was beginning to develop a 'vocabulary' for what would eventually become a network of more than 700 revolutionary public playgrounds. Eager to cultivate young imaginations and mend communities in a post-war city, van Eyck combined geometric sandpits, gently curving climbing arches and clusters of cylindrical concrete into welcoming urban spaces free from regulation and control. While the structures themselves were static, they invited unlimited, unrestricted movement. His classic 'igloo' could be climbed up, slithered down, inhabited or jumped from, while his rimmed sandpits provided seating for carers, paths to traverse, boundaries for imagined houses and so on.

In the years that followed, play sculptures' popularity mushroomed. From Pierre Székely's utilitarian French playgrounds resembling a giant's abstract clay creations to Isamu Noguchi's primary-hued geometric Playscapes (p.149) in the USA, not to mention Japan's numerous cement-moulded play objects spanning elephants, ogres and octopi, there seemed to be no limit to designers' capacity for weird and wonderful creations. The horrors and austerity of war were making way for joyful, democratic spaces where children were free to be themselves – often literally, in the case of many of van Eyck's playgrounds and the popular 'junk' or adventure playgrounds that were erected on cleared bomb sites. Unlike van Eyck's fixed schemes, these more organic playgrounds were often constructed with help from and according to the creative vision of the children who played there, with loose parts spanning scrap materials and found objects usually featuring heavily – though with a shared focus on unrestricted play.

Alas, overenthusiastic health and safety regulations put paid to the kind of visionary design that characterised post-war play spaces. These ushered in a new wave of squashy-floored, standardised and downright soulless playgrounds that would have Lady Allen

Playground in Amsterdam by Aldo van Eyck, 1964.

of Hurtwood – the children's-rights campaigner and adventure-play pioneer who famously said, 'Better a broken bone than a broken spirit' – spinning in her grave. But while today's designers will generally agree that children need to take risks, hazard assessment remains one of the biggest hurdles in creative playground design – despite plenty of research to suggest that kids are much better equipped to gauge danger than we give them credit for. Research conducted in 2017 by developmental psychologist Koraly Pérez-Edgar suggested that humans instinctively focus on threat from an early age, while a 2005 study by Tam Baillie, later Scotland's Commissioner for Children and Young People, found that 'most fatal accidents to children result from them not having learned, or not being allowed to learn, how to look after themselves.'

The Florence Experiment, p.30.

Granted, a large part of the problem is managing adult discomfort. Free-play environments, by their definition, require grown-ups to relinquish control and trust in our children's instincts. They also require designers to think entirely outside the box, since most will have a totally different perception of the environment than the kids they're designing for. Indeed, children tend to view an environment in terms of *all* the possible ways they can interact with it, while adults will generally interpret it only for its socially acceptable use. A sofa, for example, could transform into a den, trampoline, stage or obstacle course without too much imaginative input on your child's part, but to you it will never be more than somewhere to veg out (and, at a push, have a nap).

That said, age-inclusive recreational spaces appear to be having a moment. Art installations, family clubs and playful sculptures afford grown-ups the chance to connect with their inner child while connecting with their *actual* child. Believe it or not, adults also appreciate being given an opportunity to play, be it traversing a crochet tunnel suspended above an art space (p.51), exploring a monumental concrete garden (p.100) or hurtling down a slide clutching a seedling to examine how different emotions – of excitement or anxiety – affect its growth (p.30). Beyond their photogenicity (and thus, Instagram- and TikTok-friendliness), these installations transcend the boundaries of age thanks to their visual appeal, relative feeling of calm (at least, compared with the average playground) and the sense of having participated in a one-of-a-kind experience.

Cookie-cutter playgrounds have no place in a world of wildly individual children, whose disparate personalities, talents, abilities and desires demand (and deserve) so much more than the average play setup offers. Playful spaces, in any form, give children and teens the reassurance that they're welcome in public places, contrary to what many would have them believe. Play is mighty, but at the intersection of art it's a life force that has the power to transform lives, communities and cities for the better. And what sad set of swings and rusty old roundabout can say that?

Emmy Watts
London, 2024

Emmy Watts *is a London-based writer, mother and art fanatic. She has written 11 other books for Hoxton Mini Press, including* An Opinionated Guide to Kids' London *and* London's Best Playgrounds, *and is usually found in one of the capital's many inventive playscapes with her two young play enthusiasts.*

‘We don’t stop playing because we grow old; we grow old because we stop playing.’

George Bernard Shaw
(Playwright)

Play with Nature

SHANGHAI, CHINA

Its sheet-steel construction might not scream 'nature play', but this sculptural swing does a great job of showcasing the raw power of the elements. Made from a single plate split into two (one piece is round, the other angular) the interactive artwork explores conflicting extremes of emotion. Indeed, elation and fear, fragility and strength, freedom and control can be simultaneously experienced while using the swing, with extra-long chains, exposed waterfront location and surrounding hard ground posing significant risks – all while increasing the thrill. Likewise, the two steel sheets' reliance on the other for balance mirrors the delicate equilibrium of life on Earth, and human beings' constant quest for balance.

Architect: DL Atelier
Opened: 2023
Web: dl-atelier.com
Photographer: Zhu Yumeng

Urban Playground

LONDON, UK

All work and no play makes the City of London a pretty soulless place to be. In an attempt to entice families to the area and temper its stuffy image, McCloy + Muchemwa created a temporary installation that could be enjoyed by all age groups, from toddlers to tight-suited office workers. 'Carved' from a pair of sustainably made rectangular blocks, the pop-up landscape was comprised of a tantalising series of abstract 'blob' and 'block' forms primed for climbing, sliding, tunnelling and resting. Partially coated in eye-catching cornflower blue, the structures were arranged in a breadcrumb formation that enticed passers-by away from a busy road and into a leafy pedestrian square, encouraging them to take a break.

Architect: McCloy + Muchemwa
Exhibited: 2023
Web: mccloymuchemwa.com
Photographer: Luke O'Donovan

The carved blocks were inspired by traditional wooden children's toys that slot together geometrically.

Baltimore Bend Playground

ALMERE, NETHERLANDS

Almere's varied architecture and waterside location inspired the construction of this playful steel sculpture, which functions both as a stimulating playground and an attractive meeting place. Designed for use by young and old, the 115-foot artwork is deliberately ambiguous – its abstract form inviting individual artistic interpretation and imaginative playtime. Its gentle curves and azure hue are designed to draw the community as if to waves, while a series of large, circular openings serve multiple purposes: facilitating the sculpture's integration into the wider landscape, allowing parents to keep an eye on frolicking children and signposting pathways through the structure.

Designer: Studio Spass
Opened: 2022
Web: studiospass.com
Photographer: Pim Top

Breakwater

JAMESTOWN, NEW YORK, USA

Formed entirely from salvaged seven-tonne concrete wave breakers designed to protect against tides and storm surges, this minimalist sculpture-meets-playground does little to restrain the throngs that flock to play on it. Originally intended for installations at Lake Erie, the four tantalisingly arranged 'dolosse' have been coated in non-slip polyurea to encourage sitting, leaning and clambering – in stark contrast to the anti-climb paint that envelops many supposedly public sculptures.

Designers: Julia Jamrozik and Coryn Kempster
Opened: 2019
Web: ck-jj.com
Photographer: Coryn Kempster

Beatrixpark

AMSTERDAM, NETHERLANDS

A sculptural slide, a tangle of climbing ropes and floating stepping stones all feature in this concrete playscape, though all are partially hidden within its globular shell. The idea was to give visiting children a sense of autonomy by providing them with 'secret' spaces – too small for their grown-ups to access, though still with enough visibility to maintain safety. It was a revolutionary concept befitting of the spaceship-esque structure. Incorporating all the equipment into the same construction also makes for an exceptionally social space, where collaborative play and problem-solving become inevitable, whether traversing the maze of ropes, gliding on the bucket swing or incorporating the painted goalpost into a friendly kickabout.

Architect: Carve
Opened: 2016
Web: carve.nl
Photographer: Marleen Beek

Forest Loops

HAMAMATSU, JAPAN

It might resemble a child's scribble rendered in soaring tubular steel, but this striking sculptural playground is more intentional than it looks. So-called because order exists within its apparent chaos, much like an actual forest, Forest Loops is comprised of identical poles that all correspond to a ten-foot radial arc. The result is an organised mess of 'branches' that demand to be scaled – and, as a concept, present endless possibilities. Large nets traverse the lower arms, accommodating less daring ramblers and mid-climb rests –making it more enticing than even the most branch-abundant oak tree.

Architect: Suppose Design Office
Opened: 2014
Web: suppose.jp/en
Photographer: Toshiyuki Yano

La Cage aux Folles

LOS ANGELES, CALIFORNIA, USA

A 'cage for play' may well be a contradiction in terms, but this aviary-like structure that was a temporary installation in a pocket park in Los Angelese offered a great deal more freedom than its bars suggest. Formed from 346 bent steel pipes and installed by Materials and Applications, a local cultural institution, the gargantuan birdcage was designed to be explored by children as they would a jungle gym, carefully navigating a spiralling inner structure that is, at times, too narrow to be traversed by adults. Far from prison-like, the space offered a unique sanctuary for kids while at the same time it was used as a stage for mind-bending shows spanning theatre, music and performance art.

Architect: Warren Techentin
Exhibited: 2014
Web: wtarch.com
Photographer: Nicholas Allen Cope

The Florence Experiment

FLORENCE, ITALY

German artist Carsten Höller has undertaken numerous projects exploring human behaviour over the course of his 30-year career, but his Florence Experiment at Palazzo Strozzi, in collaboration with plant neurobiologist Stefano Mancuso, might quite literally be the wildest to date. Questioning how plants react to human emotions, the study invited participants to hurtle down one of Höller's iconic corkscrew slides while clutching a bean seedling. Upon disembarking, participants were asked to proceed to a pop-up laboratory where scientists monitored the effects of their emotional experience on the growth of the plant (be it ecstasy, anxiety or a combination of the two) and then to a viewing room where they watched film excerpts that corresponded to their reaction. The different volatile chemical compounds produced by audiences' respective feelings of joy and horror were then funnelled out onto the building's façade. The hope was that these would impact the direction of growth pattern of the vines that had been planted there, creating a living dialogue between art and science.

Artist: Carsten Höller
Exhibited: 2018
Photographer: Catharina Lux

The Playscape

BEIJING, CHINA

A perceived lack of traditional 'neighbourhoods' in modern Chinese cities led WAA to fabricate one for this children's community centre, recreating the street-play experience in a safe environment. Housed in a complex of 1970s industrial buildings surrounding a large courtyard, the rolling space encourages independent exploration, with giant white pipes concealing staircases and walkways that run between the outdoor and indoor play areas, while a looped rooftop terrace lets parents and carers supervise from above. The concept allows for a degree of risk usually omitted from modern playgrounds, empowering children to independently explore hidden spaces, navigate steep concrete mounds and reorientate themselves upon emerging from the covered pipes, which often span multiple floors and offer little indication of where they'll deposit visitors when they reach the other side.

Architect: WAA
Opened: 2021
Web: w-a-a.cn
Photographer: Tian Fangfang

Pipes of various sizes link the roof terraces, and below these are multiple subterranean play spaces, including netted areas and crawlspaces for toddlers.

Rocks on Wheels

MELBOURNE, AUSTRALIA

It might look comically unsafe, but appearances are deceiving at Mike Hewson's creative playscape on Melbourne's Southbank. Perched on what seem to be precarious clusters of swivel castors, 24 colossal boulders (sourced from the same quarry that supplied the city's paving stones), apparently threaten to dislodge clambering children without warning. In reality, the structures' stability is ensured through an intricate system of hidden steel rods, while the 'paving stone' flooring is actually cleverly disguised soft-fall matting. The inventive spirit of adventure playgrounds is evoked by a supposedly haphazard placement of recycled objects – hunks of twisted metal and old-school plastic playground parts secured with what looks like gaffer tape. Meanwhile, hidden toy plastic trinkets, gems and animal figures incentivise intuitive exploration. Around the wider area, smaller boulders act as breadcrumbs, inviting young explorers to stumble upon the play area themselves.

Artist: Mike Hewson
Opened: 2022
Web: mikehewson.co.nz
Photographer: Mike Hewson

The project takes its name from Diane Arbus's 1962 photograph of the same title, which depicts fake rocks being wheeled into place at Disneyland.

(Right) Hewson makes use of unexpected materials such as building offcasts and buckets, apparently serving as precarious structural support but in fact carefully engineered as part of the play area.

AMP

‘People tend to forget that play is serious.’

David Hockney
(Artist)

The Commons

COLUMBUS, INDIANA, USA

Delighting kids around the globe since 1985, late artist and architect Tom Luckey's abstract play structures are identifiable by their hovering leaf-like platforms, which look as though they've been tossed into the air and have yet to float back down. But while its perceived precariousness is an undeniable part of the draw, this vertical jungle gym is almost neurotically safe, with five thick steel columns and six miles of coated stainless steel aircraft cable keeping in place its 50 colourful podiums. Part of an indoor community space, this 35-foot structure is just one of more than 80 Luckey Climbers strewn across the globe – all custom-designed, but each as irresistibly ascendable as the next.

Architect: Tom Luckey
Opened: 2011
Web: luckeyclimbers.com
Photographer: Randy Duchaine

Net Prostoria

ZAGREB, CROATIA

A ginormous, mountable hammock might sound like a strange tenth-birthday present, but it's exactly what international design collective Numen/For Use gifted their collaborators, Croatian furniture manufacturer Prostoria, for their decennial celebration. Taking their Netko outdoor lounge chair (itself an evolution of the collective's Net sculptures) as a starting point, Numen/For Use sought to create a colossal piece of public furniture that could be inhabited by many people at once. Like the chairs, which were dotted around the pavilion for visitors to recline on, the structure consisted of a sinuous, symmetrical steel skeleton fleshed out with layers of tantalisingly springy net. While the installation provided a platform for rest and reflection, participants' experiences were predominantly playful; even when they were still, movements from other people would cause them to bounce around, resulting in a bouncy-castle-like encounter that was thoroughly befitting of a birthday party.

Designer: Numen
Opened: 2021
Web: numen.eu
Photographers: Domagoj Blažević and Vanja Šolin

The Net Prostoria was inspired by Numen's outdoor lounge chairs pictured here, utilising the same combination of bent steel and netting to create a piece of public furniture.

Uplå Stouffville

WHITCHURCH-STOUFFVILLE, CANADA

An old sugar shack affords the setting for this springy attraction, where visitors of all ages can romp among the maple trees on 9,000 square feet of elasticated nets. Reaching soaring elevations of up to 20 feet, this labyrinthine network of eye-catching ramps, tunnels and rooms is part giant trampoline, part tree-top tour, with strategically placed lookout points and diaphanous walkways enhancing the illusion of flight as you leap. At night, colourful illuminations permit nocturnal frolics, allowing visitors to experience the forest in a whole new light.

Designer: The Trekking Group
Opened: 2023
Web: on.upla.ca
Photographer: Mike Stiell

Madness is a Part of Life

TOKYO, JAPAN

Of all the possible settings for a floating crochet playground, a luxury clothing store ranked among the least likely, but then the clue was in the name for this madcap artwork. Installed in Espace Louis Vuitton Tokyo, the experiential piece by Brazilian artist Ernesto Neto explored the placement of madness in a person's life, creating feelings of instability, vertigo and elation as you traversed its woven path. Furthermore, the work touched on the theme of the human body, with participants required to keep moving through a narrow walkway as if through the digestive system, so as not to cause bottlenecks. At the end of the walkway, participants were invited to relax in a much wider structure that simulated a similarly corporeal, almost womb-like environment.

Artist: Ernesto Neto
Exhibited: 2012–13
Web: espacelouisvuittontokyo.com
Photographer: Jérémie Souteyrat

The suspended structure, created from crocheted netting and filled with plastic balls, evokes organic matter. This becomes a landscape for visitors to explore, a reminder of the continuity between the space and our own bodies.

Vårbergstoppen

STOCKHOLM, SWEDEN

Theres's more than a touch of the Indiana Jones to this dramatically sloping playscape, whose cadmium-yellow spheres appear poised to thunder down the artificial hill at any moment. Mercifully for the children who play here, the spheres, which could pass for anything from beehives to birds' nests to UFOs, are firmly rooted to the spot, housing seating, dens for hiding and even a small slide. Conceived as a series of 'little worlds', these oversized golf balls act as start and end points for winter sledging and summer climbing, as well as providing much-needed shelter in a spot that otherwise relies on trees for protection. And while there's little danger of the spheres rolling down the hill, kids are heartily encouraged to do so – by way of the seemingly endless (and Stockholm's longest) slide.

Architect: Andrén Fogelström and Land Arkitektur
Opened: 2021
Web: andrenfogelstrom.se
Photographer: Clément Morin

(Above) The gravel zone forms the heart of the play area, wide enough to accommodate gathering spots and sheltered from the weather by trees.

ForKids Club

SHENZHEN, CHINA

A lively romp through the seasons awaits visitors to this dreamy family club, where both children and adults are urged to throw off the shackles of modern life and immerse themselves in a cartoonish reimagining of the natural world. The adventure begins in leafy Spring Valley, home to a tranquil cafe and a soaring tree-like structure that affords views over all four zones. Next door, the Summer Beach invites children to ascend multi-level net bridges before plummeting via slide into a giant ball pool, all under the cover of a huge sun-like canopy. A semi-enclosed anti-gravity arena makes up Autumn Leaf, allowing kids to bounce as if weightless on a series of mini trampolines. Finally, the hibernation-focused Winter Cave offers a more subdued experience, with an open area and cosy nook serving as immersive amphitheatres for digital projections, completing the Earth's orbit of the sun.

Designer: PANORAMA Design Group
Opened: 2023
Web: panoramahk.com
Photographer: PoPo Vision

(Right) The 'Autumn' zone uses netted trampoline flooring to create a semi-enclosed, anti-gravity space.

(Opposite) The yellow 'Summer' area is deliberately tactile, with elements of rubber, plastic and rope for a rich sensory experience.

ANOHA Children's World

BERLIN, GERMANY

A giraffe bows its neck to create an exhilarating slide. Nearby, a polar bear with a sledge-framed head dangles from the ceiling, its front legs outstretched, while a giant sloth built from carpet samples lazily beckons kids to scale his reclining form. These are just three of the 150 animal sculptures that make up ANOHA's central exhibit at the Jewish Museum in Berlin – an immersive Noah's Ark designed to provoke questions around God, diversity and identity. The creatures, which all take the form of three-dimensional collages assembled from found objects and everyday items, invite diverse, sensory-rich interactions, from climbing to opening bags and boxes, and even tinkering around with musical instruments. Adjacent to the ark, a huge basin and indoor waterfall augment the flood theme, enabling kids to build and float (or sink) their own origami boats.

Architect: Olson Kundig
Opened: 2020
Web: olsonkundig.com
Photographers: Hufton & Crow,
Yves Sucksdorff and kubix Berlin

The wooden ark at the heart of ANOHA is almost 23 feet tall. Housed within a former flower market hall, the circular wooden structure compliments the curved, Brutalist ceiling overhead.

Big and Tiny Silverlake Playground

SANTA MONICA, CALIFORNIA, USA

Kids and grown-ups are equally well served at this stylish creative studio, which blends flexible childcare and co-working space in inviting, Scandinavian-style surrounds. Aimed at entrepreneurial parents seeking a healthier work–life balance, the airy space houses three thoughtfully designed areas: a calming indoor playground and creche, a dynamic adults-only workspace and a welcoming family cafe and boutique. Taking cues from the impressive rafters that make up the truss ceiling, the studio's repetitive modular scheme is evocative of a jigsaw puzzle, with recognisable two-dimensional shapes recurring across the space in the form of plywood divider screens and playful metal shelving. Likewise, the subdued palette throughout imbues the distinct areas with a feeling of serenity.

Architect: Zooco Estudio
Opened: 2018
Web: zooco.es
Photographers: Jim Newberry and Pixellab

The creche and co-working area are designed to be acoustically isolated from one another. The building is divided in two by a mirrored wall, amplifying each individual space.

MACHmit!

BERLIN, GERMANY

Elias Church (Eliaskirche) served Berlin's Prenzlauer Berg Protestant community for 90 years, but for the last 20 it's been hosting a very different congregation: hordes of frenzied children. Translating as 'join in!' in German, MACHmit! was conceived as somewhere that children of all ages and abilities could learn through experimentation and interaction. Part children's museum, part indoor playground, the space revolves around a 23-foot-high vertical maze with corridors so bewildering that there's even a lift to help parents extract their lost children. Comprised of two interconnecting structures, both open on their outer wall to afford users a view of the wider museum, the wooden maze challenges kids' problem-solving skills while offering an infinitely more visually appealing alternative to ubiquitous soft play structures.

Architect: Klaus Block
Opened: 2003
Web: machmitmuseum.de
Photographer: Karl Johaentges

‘We are never more fully alive, more completely ourselves or more deeply engrossed in anything than when we are playing.’

Charles Schaefer
(Psychologist)

nook
EXIT

Nook

ARLINGTON, VIRGINIA, USA

A 50-foot-long wooden helix play structure snakes enticingly through the centre of this family club, presenting a perspective-distorting challenge as it somersaults through the air, turning floor to wall and wall to ceiling before spitting you out the other side. Conceived as a gallery-like experience that prioritises child-led discovery, the club's open-plan space is filled with L-shaped screens – each one playing host to a different activity, from role-play stations to sensory installations. At four foot tall, the screens (or 'nooks') cocoon young children, allowing them to fully immerse themselves in their chosen task while giving adults a clear view of the wider space – particularly handy for siblings with a tendency to run in opposite directions.

Designer: Mickus Projects
Opened: 2019
Web: mickusprojects.com
Photographer: Abby Jiu

The minimalist design was intended to remove the overstimulating and chaotic elements of typical play areas, creating instead a relaxing space where children's imagination is free to roam.

Amusement Casa

KAOHSIUNG CITY, TAIWAN

A desire to maximise on family time led the owners of this playful Taiwanese home to reimagine their kitchen as a domestic destination with a focus on fun. Along with a large table where the family could gather to eat, craft and study, a dynamic play area was central to the open-plan kitchen's communal design, allowing parents and children to interact even while engaged in separate tasks. The built-in play area is focused around a charming two-storey playhouse containing a cosy reading nook and an upper deck from which kids can launch themselves down a stylish wooden slide. The slide and its adjacent swing can be fully disassembled, while the stairs that lead to the upper deck can be tucked into the floor-to-ceiling bookcase when not in use, increasing the dimensions of living space while future-proofing the home.

Designer: HAO Design
Opened: 2015
Web: haodesign.tw
Photographer: HeyCheese!

Created using mortise and tenon joints, the slide can be disassembled easily when not needed, increasing the available space on the veranda.

The 'Favourite Thing' light fixture includes backlit space for displaying items created by their daughter.

Moscow Summer House

MOSCOW, RUSSIA

Scarcity of sleep led the parents of two young children to install a multi-level play area in their minimalist Moscow summer house, inspiring their early risers to channel morning energy into play – and affording their parents an occasional lie-in. Arranged in the recess above the parents' bed, the structure incorporates an easy-climb staircase leading to two upper levels, a small wooden playhouse and swathes of white netting to prevent falls and encourage climbing and lounging – all while enabling dozing parents to keep half an eye on the kids. Downstairs, a 'secret' room hides behind a mirror – a trick that, along with the use of light wood, white walls, large windows and skylights, creates a sense of space and calm that the family deemed crucial to harmonious weekends away.

Architect: Ruetemple
Opened: 2016
Web: ruetemple.ru
Photographer: Alexander Kudimov

Doha Modern Playground

DOHA, QATAR

This visionary playscape commissioned by Qatar Museums celebrates Qatar's most architecturally significant modernist buildings; a cluster of architectural 'miniatures' reimagined for play. Created by artist Shezad Dawood with local architect and architectural historian Fatma Al Sahlawi, each structure references a different building that played a vital role in transforming Qatar into a modern, post-colonial state – and crucially, the structural quirks that imbue the project with its playful nature. The sloping Qatar Post building, for example, can be mounted and then exited via a twisted slide, while the pyramidal Doha Sheraton Hotel is interpreted as a swing set and the National Theatre & Ministry of Information's curving colonnades reimagined as a series of play tunnels. Even the playground's benches take their cues from local architecture, drawing attention the way art (and play) parallel life.

Artist: Shezad Dawood
Architect: Fatma Al Sahlawi
Opened: 2022
Web: shezaddawood.com
Photographer: Sarjoun Faour

Dawood was interested in exploring scale, reimagining famous buildings as a child-size environment. He wanted the playground to function as a 'miniature city'.

The four buildings that comprise the playground are, according to Dawood, 'a key group of modernist buildings that really represented the shift to an independent nation'. Dawood capitalised on the buildings' quirks, reinterpreting the colonnades of the National Theatre and Ministry of Information as tunnels.

Dongcheon-dong J.one Playscape

SEOUL, SOUTH KOREA

Arranged around an artificial hill, this labyrinthine play space seems to defy gravity with its Escher-like staircases and multilayered mezzanines. A mixture of textures and terrains, its neutral colours and lack of signposted areas recall the experience of playing outside while minimising the risk of injury. Children are afforded the opportunity to navigate a stimulating landscape with little to no supervision: abseiling up a hillside, wading through a ball-filled canal and traversing a cloudlike crochet canopy before whizzing back down to earth, remarkably unscathed.

Architect: Shin Architects
Opened: 2014
Web: shinarchitects.com
Photographer: Rohspace

Designed by Shin Architects, the space spreads over three levels and 3,230 square feet.

Jerry House

CHA-AM, THAILAND

If Jerry could escape Tom long enough to construct his dream home, it might resemble a giant lump of cheese – numerous holes and a continuous circulation route could enable an easy getaway when his feline nemesis inevitably caught up with him. At least, that's the concept behind this joyful beach home, which was designed to augment the holiday experience for the owners' four children. More playground than house, the property revolves around a triple-height atrium layered with five levels of net, providing a fun alternative to the main staircase that itself doubles as a thrilling play structure complete with ladders and holes for scrabbling through. There are mousehole-shaped doorways and windows that add to the glee, child-sized tunnels and ramps for sliding and a mirrored ceiling topping it all off, cultivating a sense of boundless escape and deep immersion, thoroughly befitting of a holiday home.

Architect: Onion
Opened: 2014
Web: onion.co.th
Photographer: Wison Tungthunya

(Right) Hidden at the top of the house, these beds lie either side of a tunnel that leads to the main staircase. The bed on the left is also accessible via a hole in the blue wall that opens onto to the highest net.

The house has been turned into a veritcal playground through layers of nets that are stretched across the central atrium. The nets can be used to travel from the top to the ground floor.

AirBubble Playground

WARSAW, POLAND

Concerns about pollution levels in cities inspired ecoLogicStudio to build this greenhouse-like play pavilion, which employed a pioneering micro-algae gardening system to purify its air supply. Fully sustainable, the filtration process was partially powered by play itself, with swinging ropes, bouncy spheres and water foot pumps activating the machinery that moved liquid through the bioreactors. The result was a purified microclimate for play and learning that not only eradicated air and noise pollution, but also encouraged collaborative play towards a shared objective – the small matter of ending climate change.

Architect: ecoLogicStudio
Exhibited in 2021
Web: ecologicstudio.com
Photographer: Maja Wirkus

The cylindrical timber structure is lined with 52 glass algae reactors producing a gently bubbling white noise. Their sound masks the urban noise outside, creating a calming play atmosphere.

The 52 bioreactors contain 520 litres of *Chlorella*, algae cultures that purify the air inside the pavilion each day by removing carbon dioxide and pollutants.

Jardin d'email

OTTERLO, NETHERLANDS

While not explicitly conceived as a playground, Jean Dubuffet's monumental 'garden within a garden' compels playful exploration. Inside this 6,460-square-foot concrete sculpture, visitors experience intense sensory immersion thanks to the sculpture's high perimeter wall and an uneven terrain whose peaks and valleys are only partially signposted by black contour lines zigzagging the stark white base. The result is pleasurably disorientating, allowing visitors to imagine they've entered a monochrome parallel universe, complete with abstract, black-and-white trees. Meanwhile, anyone wishing to remain in our full-colour dimension can watch the commotion unfold from an adjacent raised viewing platform.

Artist: Jean Dubuffet
Opened: 1974

La Dame du Lac

PARIS, FRANCE

Pierre Székely's La Dame du Lac was conceived for 'alpinists' (*piétons de l'espace* or 'walkers in space', as he called them), but he was adamant that the sculpture was not a mere imitation of a rock cliff. Instead, Székely's 56-foot-high, pyramidal 'lady' was made as an artistic contribution to the landscape with a strangely human form, curving gracefully among the pines. Scaling this sculpture's distinctive, ledge-embellished face is still a rite of passage for climbing enthusiasts all over the globe – despite this being prohibited for several years. More recently, the work has become a pilgrimage site for traceurs (parkour practitioners) owing to its notoriety as the purported birthplace of the precarious pastime.

Artist: Pierre Székely
Opened: 1975

La Pegaso Park

BARCELONA, SPAIN

This north Barcelona park might take its name from the 'Pegaso' (Pegasus) make of car that was once manufactured on the same grounds, but it's a betentacled mollusc (and not a winged horse) that provides the inspiration for its playground. The octopus (or 'pulpo') is an apt thematic choice, being not only the basis for the famous Galician dish but, more crucially, in possession of eight spiralling tentacles that make for outstanding slides. Accessed via a polyhedral steel frame that forms the octopus's abdomen, these gleaming chutes intertwine in a disorientating way, leaving one always a bit uncertain of precisely where they'll emerge. Encased in the pulpo's gigantic head is an equally befuddling climbing structure, with layers of net hung at various angles allowing for gravity-defying play, and a pair of rotating periscope 'eyes' enabling kids to spy on idle parents from a lofty height.

Architect: Jordi Qeralt, Richter Spielgeräte GmbH
Opened: 2019
Web: richter-spielgeraete.de

Children can observe their surroundings through two rotating periscopes – the 'eyes' of the animal.

The Brutalist Playground

LONDON, UK

Archive images of long-gone play structures from three London housing estates sparked the idea for this temporary immersive installation, which offered young visitors the opportunity to play as their grandparents once did. Despite its structures being of identical size and shape to their source material, the Brutalist Playground stood in stark contrast to the footage of the concrete originals that was projected onto the gallery walls, this time constructed from spongey, pastel-hued foam. The installation raised questions about our 'dumbing down' of children's play areas and the implications of contemporary safety measures on play, with the experience being more akin to visiting a modern soft-play centre than exploring a hard concrete playground.

Artist: Simon Terrill
Architect: Assemble
Exhibited: 2015
Web: assemblestudio.co.uk

‘The true object of all human life is play.’

G. K. Chesterton
(Philosopher)

Marmara Forum Cloud Playground

ISTANBUL, TÜRKIYE

Clouds seem a fitting choice for a rooftop playground, but these kaleidoscopic structures were actually chosen for their ability to adapt to the weather – shielding children from the sun, sheltering them from the rain and creating magic with multicoloured windows that change shade with the light. Formed from 275 hexagonal and pentagonal panels, the four play areas occupy a small rooftop plot and are designed to cater to different ages and abilities while maximising the available space. The smallest cloud affords scrambling opportunities for the youngest explorers, while the tallest poses more significant challenges, inviting older kids to ascend 26 feet skyward through a succession of nets to collect their reward: panoramic views over the city, and an exhilarating slide ride back down with an expansive forest of hammocks for sprawling.

Architect: Carve
Opened: 2020
Web: carve.nl
Photographer: Asli Dayioglu

Seventy-nine feet above street level, the playground can be found on the rooftop of the Marmara Forum shopping centre in Istanbul, Türkiye.

Superkilen

COPENHAGEN, DENMARK

Its name might mean 'giant wedge' in Danish, but Superkilen was actually designed to narrow the wedge between its local communities. Located in Copenhagen's ethnically diverse Nørrebro district, the vibrant linear park was conceived as an open-air 'world exhibition' representing each of the 60+ nationalities that call the surrounding streets home. Designers worked with local residents to source or replicate meaningful objects from all over the globe, from a star-shaped Moroccan fountain to a concrete bus stop from Kazakhstan. There's no one defined play area, but playground equipment makes up a generous chunk of the eclectic street furniture and includes a Japanese octopus slide, an Iraqi swing-bench replica and an elephant slide modelled on one found in the abandoned Ukrainian city of Pripyat.

Architect: Bjarke Ingels Group, Topotek 1, Superflex
Opened: 2012
Web: topotek1.de
Photographers: Iwan Baan and Torben Eskerod

This half-mile-long urban space is divided into three zones and colours – green, black and red – and populated by objects and sculptures from around the world that encourage play, with a plaque detailing the provenance of each object.

The Folds

CHANGZHOU, CHINA

The movement of water was the inspiration for this minimalist playscape, with a rippling surface that mimics the behaviour of ocean waves. Devised to support instinct-led, tactile play, the design trades swings and roundabouts for gentle summits and 'secret' nooks, encouraging young explorers to play as they would in nature – climbing, running, hiding and unleashing their imaginations on the blank canvas. Nooks become caves, houses and ice-cream kiosks, while peaks double as mountaintops and stages for impromptu performances. Elsewhere, yellow fencing is either fashioned into scalable structures that follow the contours of the landscape, or used to help kids ascend the smooth plastic-timber hills – and then slither down the other side.

Designer: Atelier Scale
Opened: 2020
Web: scalescape.com
Photographer: Wu Qingshan

Woods of Net

HAKONE, JAPAN

Japanese textile artist Toshiko Horiuchi MacAdam has been painstakingly crocheting playgrounds for more than 50 years. Hand-knitting may be the least conventional of ways to construct a children's play area, but inspiration struck for MacAdam when she saw a couple of kids climbing one of her sculptures and, from that day, began creating work expressly for children. Woods of Net exists as a permanent pavilion in Fuji-Hakone-Izu National Park, with a springy rainbow structure that dangles irresistibly from an inverted timber birds' nest. Assembled using the same ancient construction techniques as the wooden temples in Nara and Kyoto, the 589-piece timber dome is entirely metal-free and safeguards the nylon web from the elements. Young visitors are given the sense of being totally immersed in nature, bobbing around on an oversized hammock suspended from the forest roof.

Artist: Toshiko Horiuchi MacAdam
Architect: Tezuka Architects
Opened: 2009

Bounce Below

BLAENAU FFESTINIOG, UK

Even the most laissez-faire parents might balk at the thought of their children larking around in a Victorian slate mine, but this subterranean wonderland is far from illicit territory, having been spectacularly repurposed with play in mind – albeit only for the preposterously energetic. The brainchild of an ex-Royal Marines commando and part of the Zip World adventure park group, Bounce Below is superbly silly, comprising half a dozen huge, elasticated nets suspended across two cavern chambers – each twice the size of St Paul's Cathedral. Supplement this with neon floodlighting, high-tempo music and four industrial tunnel slides the height of two double-decker buses, and you've got yourself what might just be one of the world's most surreal play experiences.

Opened: 2014
Web: zipworld.co.uk

Wake The Tiger

BRISTOL, UK

The world's first 'amazement park' needs to be seen to be believed, but anyone who's experienced its founders' legendary Boomtown festival should have a reasonable idea of what to expect from this immersive exhibition. Built during the 2020 lockdown, which permitted a required break from frenzied festival planning, the experiential 'museum' comprises more than 40 fantastical environments, all loosely themed around solving an environmental crisis. On arrival, participants are shown around the seemingly innocuous marketing suite for a fictitious luxury apartment complex, before plunging through a portal into an alternate dimension filled with enigmatic ooze, luminescent mushrooms and talking trees (though, oddly, not a single tiger).

Opened: 2022
Web: wakethetiger.com

Balloon Museum

LONDON, UK

Wrestling 10-foot inflatable marbles, plunging chin-deep into a swimming pool filled with yellow emoji balls and partying with giant, air-filled Weebles are not standard museum pursuits, but then this wasn't your standard museum. Filling out London's 78,000-square-foot Old Billingsgate market, this blow-up bonanza addressed complex human emotions by way of 20 artist-designed installations, be it anger-management balls poised for punching, colossal cartoon faces created to tickle your funny bone or a bouncy-castle-like labyrinth that produced a potent sense of immensity. Kids were more than welcome (any serious messaging will go over younger heads) but really this was a grown-up playground, offering ample opportunity to fill up your camera roll while behaving like a child – all in the name of art.

Exhibited: 2023–24
Web: balloonmuseum.world
Photographer: David Levene

Launderette of Dreams

LONDON, UK

The routine became remarkable at this vibrant play installation, for which British-Nigerian multidisciplinary artist and designer Yinka Ilori worked with primary-age pupils from his former school, drawing inspiration from childhood visits to his local north London laundrette. Built using more than 200,000 LEGO® bricks, the arcade-like space recalled Ilori's youthful preoccupation with fantasy in the face of mundanity and featured interactive LEGO® mural walls, vending machines that dispensed LEGO® instead of soap and kaleidoscopic, toy-filled machine drums that provided an infinitely more exciting spectacle than clothes washing. The installation aimed to harness the creative optimism of youth, with young visitors also given the chance to create their own imagined worlds out of LEGO® bricks.

Artist: Yinka Ilori
Exhibited: 2021
Web: yinkailori.com
Photographer: Mark Cocksedge

YES TO
BALL GAMES

LEGO® bricks were incorporated into the installation as both construction materials and objects for play, with children invited to add to a giant LEGO® mural.

Ilori was inspired by his own experiences playing at the local laundrette while the adults were busy with laundry. 'We often forget about the mundane spaces which [provide] an opportunity for kids to meet, play and share ideas,' he said.

Pixeland

MIANYANG, CHINA

Dozens of eye-popping elements vie for attention at this multifunctional leisure space, among them an undulating climbing wave, a horse-shaped play tower and a rainbow-hued quartet of parallel slides. Based around the digital concept of pixels combining to create a bigger picture, the playscape is a patchwork of predominantly green, orange and grey squares, each hosting a different activity station. Arranged in a grid formation, tied together with an artificial sloping topography, these independent entities form a cohesive public space that appeals to all ages, with rest and performance areas interwoven with the equipment to produce a more intergenerational and inclusive landscape.

Architect: 100architects
Opened: 2018
Web: 100architects.com
Photographer: Amey Kandalgaonkar

Each of the pixels offers a different individual activity, positioned in different combinations to generate a hyper-stimulating landscape of play.

Landscape for Play

MADRID, SPAIN

Aldo van Eyck, the great Dutch architect who designed more than 700 open-ended play playgrounds in Amsterdam after WWII, was an electrifying influence on this pop-up playground's eye-catching design, which favoured sculpture-like abstract structures over standard swings and roundabouts. Madrid's flamboyant architectural landscape was another key stimulus – a choice that alluded to the relative lack of child-dedicated space in contemporary cities and, more specifically, in cultural institutions like Intermediæ Matadero, where the playscape was exhibited. As well as offering boundless play opportunities for families, the installation functioned as an inspiring setting for numerous talks and concerts during the course of the exhibition, with geometrical climbing structures, ramps and stairs doubling as playful stages and seating.

Architect: Aberrant Architecture
Exhibited: 2019
Web: aberrantarchitecture.com
Photographer: Lukasz Michalak

The Matadero exhibition hall was transformed by coloured follies, crevices and other structures without prescriptive uses that invited children to explore the space in an imaginative way.

Like Child's Play

SYDNEY, AUSTRALIA

Participants became miniatures among French conceptual artist Daniel Buren's towering geometric blocks – a playful riff on childhood games that saw us dwarfing our toys. Comprising 100 seemingly precariously perched shapes, Buren's abstract cityscape invited visitors to awaken their inner child, unlocking their creative brains as they moved from the clinically white half of the installation to the brightly coloured one, as though undertaking a psychological journey. An already bewildering sense of the surreal was amplified by way of Buren's signature striped bands, whose hypnotic effect added to the sense of being locked inside a (very weird) dream.

Artist: Daniel Buren
Exhibited: 2015–16
Web: danielburen.com

The play space's shapes and colours are inspired by the toy designs of Friedrich Fröbel, the 19th-century German pedagogue who is credited with inventing kindergarten. When exploring the landscape, visitors are encouraged to move from vivid to pure white structures.

Primary Structure

WANÅS, SWEDEN

Inside the historical grounds of Southern Sweden's Wanås Konst Park sit 104 colourful steel beams, arranged as if a three-dimensional game of Tetris has been frozen mid-level. But while the sculpture's parts are immovable, never to be slotted together into a satisfyingly complete rectangle, there are still endless interactive elements. Indeed, Jacob Dahlgren's career-long preoccupation with the relationship between body and object feels no better realised than in this minimalist playscape, which borrows its name from a 1966 exhibition at New York's Jewish Museum featuring works by Anthony Caro and Donald Judd. Both children and adults are free to climb, vault, limbo and perch on the artwork and, in doing so, become an integral part of it.

Artist: Jacob Dahlgren
Opened: 2011
Web: jacobdahlgren.com
Photographer: Mattias Givell

Noguchi Playscapes

ATLANTA, GEORGIA, USA

Renowned American artist and landscape architect Isamu Noguchi spent decades studying and designing playgrounds, describing them as 'stages for exploration' and 'primer(s) of shapes and functions; simple, mysterious, and evocative; thus educational'. Despite this career-long fascination – and multiple attempts at commissioning playgrounds in the US – this is the only permanent playground the artist realised in his lifetime. A joyful monument to Noguchi's life's work, Playscapes marries ideas from his sculptural back catalogue with concepts he'd initially explored years earlier – including a stepped swing set designed for an unrealised Hawaiian playground in 1940. Its considered arrangement of primary-coloured, geometric metal and concrete play sculptures was composed to stimulate young children's imaginations, allowing them to project their wildest fantasies onto its abstract forms.

Artist: Isamu Noguchi
Opened: 1976

Visual Playrooms, GASK

KUTNÁ HORA, CZECHIA

This vertical soft play takes its cue from Piet Mondrian's neoplastic compositions, adopting the same minimalistic visual language – but with an added third dimension. Jutting platforms tempt little ones to climb, rest and leap, inviting open-ended play through their abstract forms and primary colour palette. Part of the Central Bohemian Art Gallery (GASK)'s suite of 'visual playrooms', the play wall is an intuitive extension of Mondrian's pure forms. For kids, it's a welcome reprieve from Kutná Hora's historical attractions (it's next door to the famous Gothic cathedral of St Barbara) and a chance to expend some energy before re-joining the tourist trail.

Opened: 2010
Web: gask.art
Photographer: David Christian Lichtag

(Right and opposite) The playrooms, designed by Barbora Zachovalová, immerse visitors in famous works of art, with colourful foam blocks creating endless construction possibilities.

‘Play is the foundation of learning, creativity, self-expression and constructive problem-solving. It’s how children wrestle with life to make it meaningful.’

Susan Linn
(Writer & psychologist)

Obliteration Room

LONDON, UK

Yayoi Kusama's most interactive artwork invited participants to embrace their inner maximalist. Everyone who entered the initially clean white 'apartment' installation was handed a sheet of sticky spots with which to decorate its surfaces, transforming it over a period of weeks into a riotous rainbow of colour. Referencing the artist's preoccupation with polka dots, participatory art and accumulation, the intensely Instagrammable work offers a family-friendly alternative to her beloved infinity rooms and has appeared in more than 20 global venues over its two-decade run – a testament to its enduring popularity. Once your sticker sheet is empty, you're welcome to make yourself at home among the dots, jumping on the beds, battling friends at table football and otherwise submerging yourself in Kusama's vibrant world.

Artist: Yayoi Kusama
Exhibited: 2022
Web: yayoi-kusama.jp

The domestic environment – sofas, dining table and chairs – was painted completely white, functioning as a blank canvas to be 'obliterated' by brightly coloured dots.

Tubo

HANGZHOU, CHINA

The simple pleasure of colouring inspired this equally simple installation, which swapped paper and pens for perforated surfaces and colourful foam tubes. Just as they would with a new colouring book, children could let rip on a series of blank canvases – only in this case they were three-dimensional, taking the form of 16 giant food-shaped structures including a carrot, a shrimp and a banana, as well as a surrounding 'pinboard' wall. The flexible tubes could be slotted and tied through the holes, filling them with colour that could either be true to the object the structure depicted or totally fantastical, eventually creating a 'furry food' installation to be pulled apart and recoloured infinite times.

Artist: Mathery Studio
Exhibited: 2015
Web: mathery.it

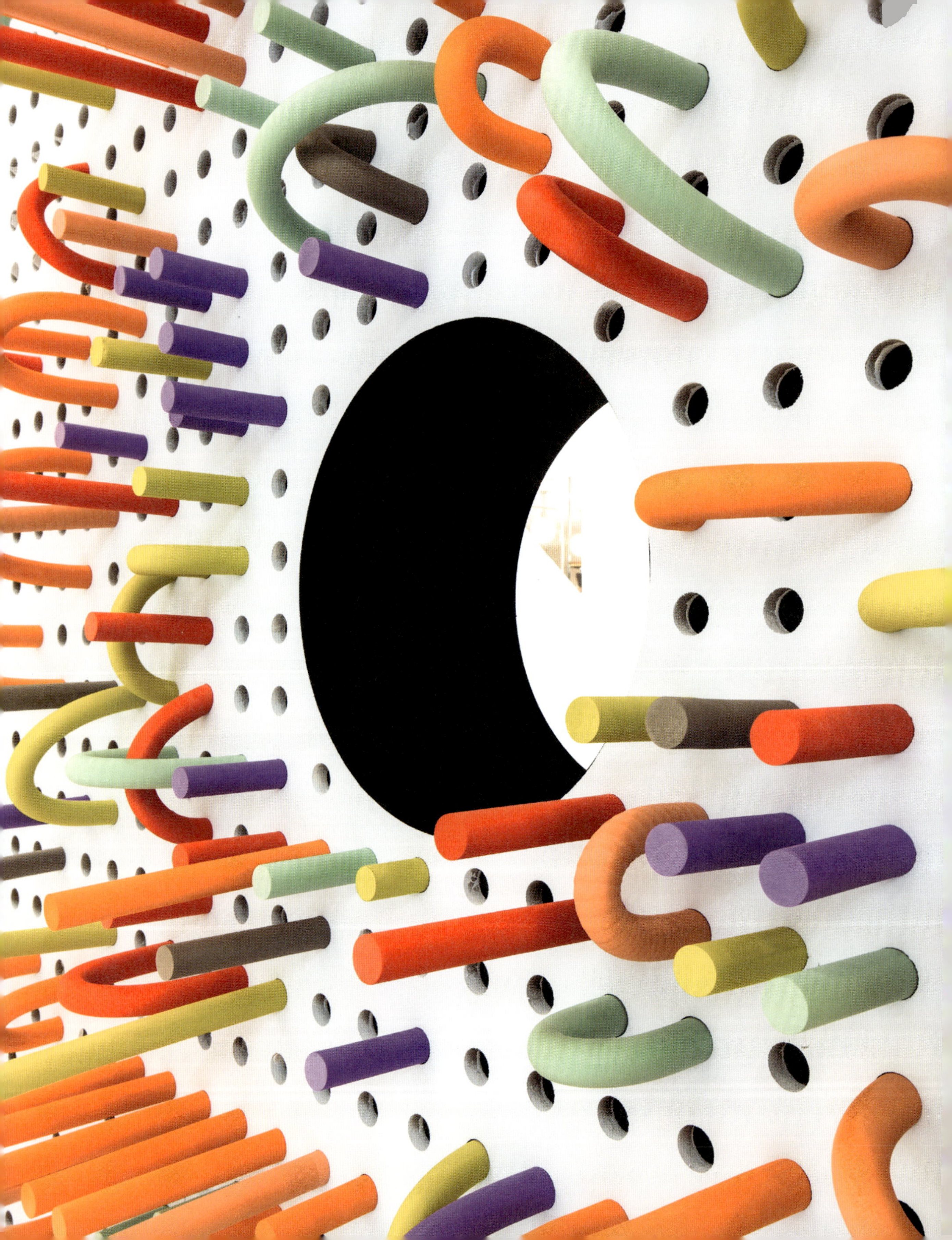

Children were encouraged to 'colour' the space by filling the holes of the blank sculptures with vibrant foam tubes.

Dorr Kids Playground

NAMYANGJU CITY, SOUTH KOREA

Tired of warning your kids not to climb up the slide? At this indoor playground, you don't have to, thanks to an ingenious circular structure that allows multiple riders to soar and dive in tandem without risk of collision. Elsewhere, a fortress wall invites gentle battle play, encouraging collaboration and emotional regulation, while the almost totally white colour scheme is more in keeping with a restful yoga studio than a hectic playground. Indeed, Maum Studio appear to have completely dispensed with the playground rulebook, creating a tantalisingly rebellious antithesis to a standard soft play. Inside, children become players in both senses, as though the monochrome furniture were a mere stage on which to project the content of their imaginations, infusing it with colour and creativity.

Designer: Maum Studio
Opened: 2021
Web: maumstudio.co.kr
Photographer: Ju Yeon Lee

Deliberately monochromatic, the play area is only brought to vibrant life when filled with the movements and play of children.

Swarovski Kristallwelten Playtower

WATTENS, AUSTRIA

A glass-clad tower might not be the most obvious backdrop for a children's soft play, but then Swarovski's Kristallwelten is no ordinary theme park. The newest of the experiential wonderland's many spectacles, the outwardly crystalline Playtower packs in springy trampolines, floating stepping stones and a 46-foot vertical play net across four levels, encouraging play experiences such as climbing, swinging, sliding and even seemingly floating in mid-air. The tower joins established delights including a waterfall-spewing giant's head, home to an 18-room Chamber of Wonder; a hedge maze built to resemble the giant's hand; and an extravagant Jaime Hayon-designed monochrome carousel studded with 15 million Swarovski crystals.

Architect: Snøhetta
Opened: 2014
Web: old.snohetta.com
Photographer: Patrick Lüth

Jaime Hayon's monochrome carousel is studded with 15 million Swarovski crystals.

Olioli

DUBAI, UAE

Nothing lights up the brain like play. At least, that's the mantra shared by National Institute for Play founder Dr Stuart Brown and this STEM-focused children's museum, with a name that means 'joy' in Hawaiian. Drawing inspiration from children's museums, art galleries and innovative playgrounds, as well as creative labs and maker spaces, this purpose-built warehouse of wonders stimulates open-ended, inquisitive play across 40 engaging activities and eight cutting-edge galleries, from washing cars in the Water Gallery to making music in the Future Park. The most brain-illuminating installation, however, has to be Toshi's (AKA textile artist Toshiko Horiuchi MacAdam's) Nets (p.122) – a colourful crochet playground designed for bouncing, relaxing and (actually very safe) risky play.

Architect Sneha Divias Atelier
Artist: Toshiko Horiuchi MacAdam
Opened: 2017
Web: snehadivias.com

The Nest

CHONGQING, CHINA

Play is for everyone. At least, that's the thinking behind this cross-generational public intervention. Such age-inclusivity may well be pioneering but it's unlikely to be the first thing you notice about 100architects' playscapes, which blend highly imaginative, narrative-led structures with eye-popping colour. The multifunctional Nest offers recreation and relaxation for everyone from pre-schoolers to pensioners, with elements including a sunken sandpit, fitness area, Chinese chess table and senior citizens' exercise equipment. The avian trio, along with the giant red 'worm' slide and connecting scrambling tunnel, provide the visual focus, while a winding running track knits everything together – and functional lighting encourages use well into the small hours.

Architect: 100architects
Opened: 2021
Web: 100architects.com
Photographer: Rex Zou

RUN

HIGH MUSEUM OF ART

Tiovivo

ATLANTA, GEORGIA, USA

A colourful menagerie of reimagined animals and objects made up Jaime Hayon's temporary Tiovivo, or 'carousel', installation at Atlanta's High Museum of Art. Equipped with diminutive child-sized doorways and slides, the hollow structures invited hands-on discovery while acting as an extension of the gallery space, inspiring an early appreciation of art. Vaguely porcine and simian silhouettes were rendered even more abstract through the application of playful chevron, stripe and polka-dot patterns, further blurring the line between art and play.

Artist: Jaime Hayon
Exhibited: 2016–17, High Museum of Art, Atlanta
Web: hayonstudio.com
Photographer: Jonathan Hillyer

The four wooden sculptures are designed in the shapes of animals or familiar objects, with child-sized openings that encourage interaction.

Montessori Kindergarten

BEIJING, CHINA

A quaint, village-like layout was chosen for this Montessori nursery school, with a view to building a safe, familiar environment over which attending children felt a sense of ownership. Designed according to their physical proportions, the scaled-down space encompasses child-sized house structures, an open-plan 'town square' with a large indoor tree and a river-like blue ombre staircase that courses from floor to floor. This idea of children immersing themselves in the natural world (albeit a simulated one) is central to the Montessori philosophy, as is a minimalistic use of colour and embellishment, all combining to create a zen-like mood that's highly conducive to learning.

Architect: ArkA
Opened: 2017
Web: myarkadesign.com
Photographer: Chiara Ye

‘Play is the work of the child.’

Maria Montessori
(Educator)

Landscape Alley

KYIV, UKRAINE

It doesn't take a Mad Hatter to fathom the theme of this interactive sculpture park, whose idiosyncratic playground is populated by a fancifully dressed white rabbit, an upturned top hat and a cat with a maniacal grin. Perched on a hill above Kyiv, Landscape Alley houses around 75 Wonderland-worthy mosaic works – the majority created by local artist Kostiantyn Skrytutskyi and funded by donations from local residents and charities. But while the sculptures are as extraordinary as Alice's adventures, their location is arguably even more so: built on both the remains of Ukraine's first stone church and Kyiv's oldest pagan temple, there's even an ancient tree said to grant wishes. Truly a magical place worth treasuring.

Artist: Kostiantyn Skrytutskyi
Opened: 2009

The alley was initially intended as a viewing point for Kyiv's Dnieper River, but was transformed in 2009 by playful mosaic sculptures that double up as slides, climbing apparatus and seating areas.

Miffy Museum

UTRECHT, NETHERLANDS

Miffy's creator, Dick Bruna, memorably said, 'I don't want to be prescriptive. I want children to have fun.' This laudable sentiment, along with the simple, graphic line-work and limited palette of bold, solid colours found in his picture books, provides the inspiration for this interactive museum for pre-schoolers and toddlers, ages two to six. Inside, fans of the beloved white bunny are invited to experience 'the world in miniature', discovering 12 immersive learning environments with themes selected for their cultural value and relatability to children. Here, kids can learn about road safety at the traffic square or about colours and shapes at the farm, while a mix of mechanical and sensory displays create as interactive – and memorable – an experience as possible.

Architect: Soda
Opened: 2016 (expanded in 2023)
Web: soda.nl

Spaces inside the museum are inspired by Dick Bruna's picture books, with interactive exhibits where children can visit Miffy in her own home, go to the doctor, explore the zoo and learn more about museums.

nijntje
museum

Blazing Battle of the Dragon

DUBAI, UAE

Its medieval narrative may seem oddly incongruous with Dubai's glistening skyscrapers, but this ambitious playground by prolific playground designers Monstrum more than matches the drama of its modern surroundings. Here, in the heart of the city's largest public green space, children of all ages can test their dragon-slaying mettle, scrambling up the vast beast's back, scaling its wings via handy footholds or bravely penetrating its belly through a conveniently placed cubby hole and hastily shooting out from its jaws in a bolt of flames. Meanwhile, less audacious adventurers can seek shelter in the adjacent stronghold while plotting their escape via the rickety bridge or soaring slide. Either way, this one's not for the faint of heart.

Architect: Monstrum, Insite Landscape Archtects
Opened: 2019
Web: monstrum.dk

Kraken

SHENZHEN, CHINA

A friendly octopus in a beanie hat may be not quite how you picture the kraken, the mythological monster with a penchant for sinking ships. But then, its creator Dutch artist Florentijn Hofman isn't exactly known for his seriousness, previously taking the opportunity to instal giant rubber ducks and a cartoonish hippopotamus in city rivers. Indeed, while the cephalopod might have taken up residence by its adopted city's harbour, it definitely has no plans to hijack any vessels – instead inviting children to clamber aboard its body via one of its tentacles. Brave buccaneers can then shimmy up ropes or climb stairs towards its head, stopping to explore a giant, crocheted maze before hurtling back down a tentacle slide.

Artist: Florentijn Hofman
Architect: UAP
Opened: 2017
Web: uapcompany.com

Children can climb up the creature's tentacles, through a netted expanse and into a play space contained inside its rounded head.

Animal Factory

AMSTERDAM, NETHERLANDS

Children's tendencies to use simple, universal signs in their drawings inspires much of toy designer Luca Boscardin's work – his menagerie of minimalist animal play structures being perhaps his most effective design to date. Produced to the exact size and proportions of the creatures they represent, Boscardin's metal structures allowed children and adults to imagine they were encountering real animals when standing at certain angles, while appearing to be something entirely different to others. Fully open to interpretation, the animals represented different things to different people: a racing-green crocodile became a balance beam for a child or an aerobic stepper for an adult, while a lemon-yellow giraffe presented both climbing and pull-up opportunities. Beyond accommodating play and exercise, the creatures could be used as bike racks, seating and teen hangouts, with the option of adding infinite animals to the herd.

Artist: Luca Boscardin
Exhibited: 2021, 2022
Web: lucaboscardin.com
Photographer: Tim Stet

inkids x LINE FRIENDS Playground

BEIJING, CHINA

A menagerie of cute critters inhabits this colossal shopping centre-located soft play, injecting pops of colour into the otherwise startlingly white space. Created by South Korean designer Kang Byeong Mok in 2011, the LINE FRIENDS gained immense popularity across East Asia and the US, and lend their names to different areas of the forest- and ocean-themed playground: the Leonard Pond is peppered with lily pads, while the Edward Waterfall consists of a spiralling white slide leading into a bubbling stream of balls. In keeping with the characters' squishy forms, the designers have eschewed harsh angles in favour of smooth curves and arches, inspired by the trajectory of a bouncing ball. Overhead, a cloudlike netted mezzanine doubles the playable space, ensuring the sky is the limit for energetic young visitors.

Designer: Studio OKGO
Opened: 2017

inKIDS WITH LINE FRIENDS

The 9,500-square-foot play space inside a shopping centre focuses on fostering an enjoyment of 'the world beneath your feet', with nature-inspired elements such as giant lily pads, mountainous rock climbing and a ballpit lake.

LEO
POND

St Paul's School

LONDON, UK

Is it a pirate ship? Is it a spacecraft? Is it a giant spider? This suspended playground's theme is deliberately slippery, empowering children to project their own ideas onto its structure, becoming pirates one day, astronauts the next and a colony of fire ants swarming a tarantula the day after that. Such ambiguity is particularly suited to a school playground, given that the same children will play on it daily and would quickly tire of a prescribed theme. Still, it's the structure's floating central arrangement that affords the most scope for imaginative play. The frame is suspended from concrete pillars and makes use of the entire vertical space, permitting movement from floor to ceiling via stepping stones and rope ladders and back down again using the slide, in a never-ending flow of activity.

Architect: Kilburn Nightingale Architects, Play Equip
Opened: 2022
Web: playequip.com
Photographer: Lewis Allen

The structure is designed with multiple access and exit routes, from a slide to a fireman's pole, and also includes thick rope, wooden benches for seating and netting to scramble up.

Moku-Yama

ONTARIO, CANADA

Clusters of seemingly ordinary cedar cylinders create endless play scenarios in this undulating playscape, whose name means 'wood mountain' in Japanese. Each of the structure's cylinders is almost invisibly connected to the next, creating an illusion of floating hills and valleys when climbed over, or a network of caves with stalactites when approached from below. As well as presenting virtually infinite role-play prospects for younger ones, the structure offers tantalising risky play opportunities for older children. Meanwhile, often-ignored teens can congregate on the taller 'trunks', while adults will appreciate the aesthetic beauty of the arrangement.

Architect: Kengo Kuma & Associates, Earthscape
Opened: 2023
Web: kkaa.co.jp

Nia School

MEXICO CITY, MEXICO

Sitting still isn't an option at this Mexico City school – at least, it would be a pity given the infinite opportunities for movement afforded by its play areas. Devised according to Montessori philosophy, the largely wooden landscape incites free movement, self-directed learning and independent problem-solving. Floating pathways, suspended monkey bars and alluring climbing walls and tunnels comprise just a handful of its creative apparatus. Natural – or seemingly natural – materials help to emulate the experience of playing outside, with beanbag chairs that resemble rocks, hexagonal rugs designed to look like geometric basalt and slices of oak that act as handholds, while the decision to round off edges creates a reassuringly safe environment.

Architect: Sulkin Askenazi
Opened: 2019
Web: sulkinaskenazi.com
Photographer: Aldo C Gracia

(Right) The 6,450-square-foot space includes an outdoor learning area, connected to the classroom by a floor-to-ceiling window.

The classroom is fitted with materials such as cork and oak wood to create a soft, tactile environment.

Skyscraper Indoor Playground

TEL AVIV, ISRAEL

Tree-like columns, towering treehouse structures and a carpet of sea blue and forest green would fool you into believing this 15th-floor playscape was a woodland wonderland – at least, were it not for the views of the Tel Aviv skyline afforded by its floor-to-ceiling windows. Located in the headquarters of an international software company, this nature-inspired playground was designed to foster a sense of community among employees by providing a restful space for them to relax with other families. Here, children are not only welcomed into a traditionally adult domain; they're encouraged to play as though roaming in the wild, honing their scrambling skills on the climbing wall, taking a break on one of the swinging hammocks and reaping the benefits of outdoor play inside an urban high-rise.

Artist: Sarit Shani Hay
Opened: 2022
Web: shanihay.com
Photographer: Roni Cnaani

SKIU 236919 12

Phorms Schoolyard

BERLIN, GERMANY

The eternally versatile shipping container lies at the heart of the KuKuk Box – a customisable, modular playscape designed to entertain all age groups. Installed at Berlin's bilingual Phorms School for 4–18-year-olds, the elegant KuKuk takes the form of two multi-storey 'houses' linked in mid-air via crawl tunnel – a scattering of open 'windows' offering the only glimpse of what lies within. As well as being weatherproof, the 'containerscape' gives students a uniquely social and independent play experience, packed with opportunities for exploration, role-play and collaboration for younger children, from climbing to sand play and even drawing on its chalkboard walls. With its easy conveyance and assembly, the KuKuk is also optimised for use in crisis regions such as refugee camps.

Architect: KuKuk Box
Opened: 2023
Web: kukuk-box.com
Photographer: HEJM Foto

Space limitations in the schoolyard meant that the playground could only occupy a small area, so the boxes have been designed to create a vertical landscape rather than a horizontal one.

The play space suits children of multiple ages, with wooden climbing facilities inside each box for younger children to clamber, play and hide among, while also providing spaces for older children to relax and socialise undisturbed.

Five Fields Play Structure

LEXINGTON, MASSACHUSETTS, USA

Ambiguity is central to the success of this distinctive structure, which was designed to encourage collaborative play among children living in a close-knit neighbourhood. Situated on common land that has been maintained by residents since the 1950s, the singular, house-like construction capitalises on the site's already robust sense of community spirit, with diverse elements such as zip wires, vertical tubes and hidden rooms designed to challenge kids of all ages and stages of development. It's irresistibly non-prescriptive, with subtle, abstract graphics indicating only the various concealed entrances, leaving children free to explore the empty 'rooms' that serve as a backdrop to almost any game imaginable.

Architect: Matter Design, FR|SCH Projects
Opened: 2016
Web: matterdesignstudio.com
Photographer: Brandon Clifford

‘Play is the highest form of research.’

Albert Einstein
(Physicist)

Playville

BANGKOK, THAILAND

Thailand's unpredictable climate inspired the creators of this Bangkok play centre to 'bring the outdoors in', creating a nature-themed oasis that feels welcoming whatever the weather. Comprising four distinct areas themed around naturally occurring phenomena, Playville aims to safely mimic a toddler's experience of exploring in nature. Different terrains encourage children to experiment with their bodies, climbing, diving and crawling as they see fit, while raised structures invite inquisitive exploration both over and under. A strong focus on natural light was central to realising the concept, with muted colours used throughout, multiple skylights to attract the sun and a curtain of loosely threaded felt pieces on the glass façade allowing scattered light to filter through as they move – all working to intensify the sense of playing outdoors.

Architect: Nitaprow
Opened: 2018
Web: nitaprow.com
Photographer: Ketsiree Wongwan

(Above) Climbing and sliding is possible on the raised wooden platform, while the space beneath it becomes an intimate hideaway.

The Event of a Thread

NEW YORK CITY, NEW YORK, USA

Pigeons cooed, swings soared, children shrieked delightedly. Ann Hamilton's most famous performance piece became, as she observed, 'like a park' – but then your average park doesn't usually involve caped performers reading from literary texts while members of the public listen through speakers wrapped in paper bags. The joyful, carefree spirit of a park was recreated during the work's month-long run in the Armory's cavernous Drill Hall, where the movements of 42 wood-plank swings dictated those of an immense silk curtain, courtesy of a meticulously engineered system of ropes and pulleys. While some experienced the thrill of flying through the air on swings suspended from the hall's 85-foot ceiling, others lay beneath the curtain, enjoying it billow above them. It created a feeling of community beyond what Hamilton had predicted, with many participants choosing to linger in the hall for hours at a time.

Artist: Ann Hamilton
Exhibited: 2012
Web: annhamiltonstudio.com
Photographer: Thibault Jeanson

Thomas Dambo's trolls

GERMFASK, MICHIGAN, USA

Thomas Dambo's sculptures are total rubbish. Hundreds of tonnes of it, in fact. A self-styled 'environmental art activist', Dambo has devoted his life to creating treasure out of trash, upcycling everything from fallen tree debris to discarded shipping pallets to create his charismatic troll army, which can be found in natural landscapes all over the world. While some are depicted engaged in activities – playing instruments, watching the clouds, piling stones – and not necessarily conceived as play structures, these sustainable giants are certainly playful, even in spite of their serious message. One troll in Dambo's native Denmark dangles a fishing rod that doubles as a rope swing; another in Colorado's allows access to the adjacent lake via his beard; while a third in Chicago appears to catch children in a rudimentary trap. The artist's fascination with trolls is partly a reference to Old Norse folklore, but he also sees the giants as 'protectors of the environment' and a metaphor for nature's unpredictability.

Artist: Thomas Dambo
Opened: 2014
Web: thomasdambo.com

Nishi-Rokugō Koen

TOKYO, JAPAN

It might be half a century old and constructed almost entirely from worn-out rubber tyres (sourced from the nearby Kawasaki manufacturing plants) but there's nothing tyre-d about this iconic playground. Opened just 15 years after the release of the original 1954 Godzilla film, the 40,000-square-foot park is best known for two towering tyre monsters, which stand at five and eight feet tall respectively, with the larger housing a tunnel in its colossal tail. Climbing the Godzillas is prohibited these days but there's still plenty of fun to be had in this sandy-bottomed playground, where 3,000+ tyres have been recycled into all manner of swings, tube slides, stepping stones and bouldering holds – plus plenty of loose tyres reserved for fashioning your own prehistoric, reptilian goliaths.

Opened: 1969

Parque Gulliver

VALENCIA, SPAIN

At 230 feet long and 30 feet high, this epic fibreglass recreation of a sleeping Gulliver allows children (and brave grown-ups) to play out the satirical tale of Gulliver's Travels, in which a sleeping Gulliver is tied to the ground by minute Lilliputians. Parque Gulliver was opened in 1990, and lies within Valencia's Jardí del Túria, a four mile-long urban park occupying what was once the riverbed of the River Turia, before it was diverted to the south of the city in 1957. The open-play possibilities here are virtually endless – scrambling up the giant's limbs, hurtling down one of the many slides that form his hair and clothing, exploring the numerous ropes, cargo nets and slides of varying gradients. The sculpture appeals to children of all ages and abilities, and also conceals a brilliantly meta surprise: a scale model of itself tucked inside Gulliver's hat.

Architect: Rafael Rivera
Artist: Manolo Martín
Opened: 1990

(Below) There are multiple slides and stairways hidden around Gulliver's enormous body, with the steepest slides found among the strands of his hair.

La Laguna Park

SAN GABRIEL, CALIFORNIA, USA

Mexican concrete artist Benjamin Dominguez was virtually unheard of when he constructed his lagoon-themed playscape in San Gabriel's now-legendary Vincent Lugo Park. Often called 'Dinosaur Park' due to the misidentification of its resident sea-serpent slide, La Laguna was saved from demolition 40 years after its construction thanks to the enthusiastic fundraising efforts of a generation of adults who grew up near the park. Now listed on the California Register of Historic Places, the playground's 14 cement structures are still very much in use 60 years down the line, with Minnie the whale slide, Ozzie the octopus climber and their friends among some of the best-loved and most-recognised playground structures on the planet.

Artist: Benjamin Dominguez
Opened: 1965

Toa Payoh Dragon Playground

TOA PAYOH, SINGAPORE

Seemingly immortal, Toa Payoh's dragon playground has outlived almost all of its contemporaries – not to mention the apartment block it was built to serve. Constructed as part of a series of playgrounds themed around local heritage and culture, the 50-year-old landmark has endured the test of time – in part due to its sturdy construction, but largely thanks to the community that its designer hoped it might unite. One of the few remaining dragon playgrounds in Singapore, a popular design that was phased out in the 1990s due to safety concerns, the structure invites a one-way journey where children travel from tail to head along a serpentine body comprising multicoloured steel rainbow rings, before slithering down one of two concrete slides hidden inside its majestic mosaic head.

Architect: Khor Ean Ghee
Opened: 1979

Lily Floating Playground

POITIERS, FRANCE

Not content with the thrill of springing around on a regular, fixed trampoline, the creators of French amusement park Futuroscope installed a floating trampoline park on its central lake. Arranged across five enormous 'lily pad' buoys attached to a 130-foot ring-shaped deck, its 20 circular springboards elicit all the excitement of a trampoline park with the added precariousness of water, with unpredictable movements that gently displace the buoys while allowing them to drift in response to jumpers' leaps. Visitors are invited to spring from pad to pad, utilising the connecting mesh bridges to explore different buoys, or simply to lie back and relax while the installation sways beneath them.

Architect: WAO Architecture
Opened: 2019
Web: wild.paris
Photographer: Sergio Grazia

Lolly-Laputan

DALIAN, CHINA

A child's drawing of an imagined 'Fairy Land' informed the design of this dreamlike kids' cafe, whose castle-in-the-clouds playscape is a veritable heaven for both children and grown-ups. Rendered using a limited palette that avoids overstimulation and promotes play without limits, Lolly-Laputan's play area is set within a 'Cloudy Town' characterised by undulating layers of white acrylic and featuring tree houses made of white net, gleaming slides and a monochrome ball pit. A white and gold carousel provides a minimalist yet fully functional twist on the fairground favourite, while a golden 'castle' dining area encourages the prioritisation of mealtimes and well-stocked supermarket and kitchen role-play zones mimic real-world scenarios while preserving the fantasy aesthetic.

Architect: Wutopia Lab
Opened: 2019
Web: wutopialab.com

Play areas are designed to be educational as well as fun, with activities to develop children's social and motor skills.

Plants vs Zombies

WUXI, CHINA

It might take its inspiration from a wildly addictive computer game, but this eye-catching playscape urges kids to ditch the screens and embark on a real-life adventure. Designed in close collaboration with video game company EA, the Plants vs Zombies playground is dominated by a 25-foot zombie robot that children are tasked with defeating, entering its body via its legs and ascending five levels to overthrow the evil Dr Zomboss who controls the monster from above, before shooting back down to earth via its twirling arm-slides. Here at ground level, visitors will encounter another gaggle of – albeit much smaller – zombies reenacting a scene from the game's Pirate Seas world. Like all Monstrum playgrounds, it's entirely unrestricted, inviting spontaneous movement in an outstandingly inspiring landscape.

Architect: Monstrum
Opened: 2018
Web: monstrum.dk

The Golem

JERUSALEM, ISRAEL

It may look like the stuff of nightmares, but this three-tongued colossus has been beloved by the youngsters of Jerusalem's Kiryat HaYovel neighbourhood for more than half a century. Constructed in 1972 by celebrated French sculptor Niki de Saint Phalle at the request of the city's then-mayor Teddy Kollek, the Golem was originally condemned by the city council as too frightening for children, but later approved upon the artist's insistence that scary things allow children to conquer their fears. The sprayed concrete play sculpture has been helping kids to quite literally face their demon(s) ever since, surviving five decades of extremely enthusiastic use – not to mention the partial destruction of the surrounding park – thanks to an unwaveringly devoted community and dedicated restoration programme that will, with any luck, see kids shooting from its gaping jaws for at least another 50 years.

Artist: Niki de Saint Phalle
Opened: 1972

Ku.Be House of Culture and Movement

COPENHAGEN, DENMARK

Much more than just an indoor playground, this innovative community space is so deeply committed to getting visitors moving that even routes around the building encourage wiggles, slides, hops and skips. At one end, a pair of perplexing vertical mazes, a firefighter's pole, a net tunnel and a hulking tube slide offer exhilarating transitions between floors, challenging motor skills and sheer nerve. Elsewhere, an alluringly smooth concrete climbing wall beckons guests upwards, using a fixed rope or a smattering of bright-red footholds, and down again via one of several carved-out slides. While these playful elements are for the most part utilised by children, adults are urged to incorporate them into their visit too – perhaps in between the yoga, parkour or dance classes that Ku.Be also host.

Architect: MVRDV and ADEPT
Opened: 2016
Web: mvrdv.com
Photographer: Ossip van Duivenbode

Konditaget Lüders

COPENHAGEN, DENMARK

Multi-storey carparks aren't known for their beauty, but this public park – built on the roof of a parking structure – is a breathtaking exception to the rule. Set 80 feet above ground, the impressive recreational space was designed to enhance the visual appeal of an otherwise unremarkable building, as well as augmenting its functionality. Here, adult exercise equipment is arranged alongside children's play apparatus, from swings and climbing frames to a series of sunken trampolines and red mounds that give the landscape an almost Martian character. Access is via eight flights of stairs set into the building's green-walled façade, though that only amplifies the payback at the top, when successful climbers are rewarded with panoramic views of Nordhavn Harbour.

Architect: JAJA Architects
Opened: 2016
Web: jaja.archi
Photographer: Rasmus Hjortshøj/Coast Studio

Red Dunes

GUANGZHOU, CHINA

Is there life on Mars? This space-age playscape invites children of all ages to find out, navigating rolling red dunes, hidden caves and spacecraft-like playhouses (even coming face-to-face with a giant panda) for a delightfully unearthly play experience. Set around an undulating, multi-level concrete construction, the playground incorporates distinct areas for different age groups while encouraging collaborative play through synergistic design. Less confident climbers can easily scale gently sloping hills, while more experienced hikers brave the steeper sections with a little help from conveniently placed holds and ropes. The large, covered central area increases the playable space while appealing to everyone from tots to teens. The designers' commitment to sustainability is also realised through minimal material consumption and a natural drainage system, creating a decidedly thoughtful space.

Architect: Xisui Design
Opened: 2023
Web: xisuidesign.com
Photographer: Yihao Hu

Shenzhen Nai'erbao Family Center

SHENZHEN, CHINA

This fantastical play space imagines a city inhabited entirely by children, with a dreamlike aesthetic of pastel hues, clashing patterns, giant parasols and joyfully designed, bubble-shaped 'buildings'. Within these are different role-play opportunities, inviting children to partake in seemingly mundane pastimes such as going for pizza and even visiting the dentist. Designed to fill a shopping mall atrium, the playscape takes the form of a futuristic 'city in the sky', with transparent slides and corridors enabling movement between the upper floors, and ride-on cars for exploration at ground level, leaving no one in doubt that this is a land of pure imagination.

Architect: X+Living
Opened: 2019
Web: xl-muse.com
Photographer: SFAP

DrESSING Room

DENTAL
CLINIC
NEOBIO
JUMP

Located inside a shopping centre, parents can eat at the adjoining restaurant while their children play.

(Opposite) Designed to be a miniature, child-sized city, the play space even includes toy cars with their own designated parking spaces outside pretend shops.

City Museum, St. Louis

ST LOUIS, MISSOURI, USA

Such a generic designation does little justice to this eccentric family destination, whose mind-blowing exhibits largely comprise salvaged industrial objects repurposed as unconventional play installations. Constructed over four years by sculptor Bob Cassilly and his 20-strong team of artists, this vast palace of delights occupies an outdoor play area, roof and four interior floors of a former shoe factory, with original interior structures like a repurposed shoe chute forming the basis of some of its wildly popular attractions. Inside, visitors navigate a labyrinthine network of hand-sculpted 'caves', discover a 'skateless skate park' and tumble down a motley assortment of more than 30 slides. Outside, the madcap MonstroCity sculpture invites the pluckiest explorers to scramble through giant Slinkies made of old refrigerating coils and board aircraft fuselages that appear to float in mid-air, while a precariously balanced (and fully boardable) school bus looks ready to plunge right off the roof.

Artist: Bob Cassilly
Opened: 1997
Web: citymuseum.org

Children can climb aboard the school bus, apparently balanced precariously over the edge of the building.

The Rampart Wave

LYON, FRANCE

Perched on the site of a former military barracks, this largely vertical playscape is notable for its 23-foot-high wall – a feature that references the story of 19th-century rampart attack when stampeded by children. Designed to encourage independent, collaborative and at times risky play, the outwardly minimalistic wooden playscape conceals a network of passageways so complex, there's with no way of knowing where they go, or which alcove leads to which entrance. Children are compelled to form an 'army', working together to reach the top of the rampart before sliding back down to regroup and formulate their next plan of attack.

Architect: BASE Landscape Architecture
Opened: 2014
Web: baseland.fr

Children can scale the 23-foot-high wall using footholds and ropes, climbing through alcoves leading to different internal areas.

Image credits

4 top image ©Masaki Koizumi, courtesy Toshiko Horiuchi MacAdam studio, bottom image ©BASE; 7 ©The Amsterdam City Archive; 8 ©Mauritius images GmbH; 13 ©Zhu Yumeng, courtesy DL Atelier; 14–17 ©Luke O'Donovan; 18 ©Pim Top for Arttenders x Studio Spass; 21 ©Coryn Kempster and Julia Jamrozik; 22 ©Marleen Beek for Carve; 25 ©Toshiyuki Yano; 26–29 ©Nick Cope; 31 ©Mauritius images GmbH; 33–35 ©Tian Fang Fang, Courtesy of WAA; 37–39 ©Mike Hewson; 43 ©Randy Duchaine / Alamy Stock Photo; 44–47 ©Numen/Foruse, photography by Domagoj Blažević and Vanja Šolin; 48 ©Mike Stiell; 50–53 ©Jérémie Southeyrat; 54–57 ©Clément Morin, courtesy Land Arkitektur; 59–61 ©PoPo Vision, images courtesy PANORAMA Design Group; 63 ©kubix Berln ; 64 top ©Hufton & Crow, bottom ©Yves Sucksdorff / Jüdisches Museum Berlin; 65 ©Hufton & Crow; 67 ©Jim Newberry; 68 ©Pixellab; 71 ©Karl Johaentges/Lookphotos; 74–77 ©Abby Jiu; 79–81 ©HeyCheese!; 82–83 ©Alexander Kudimov; 85–87 ©Sarjoun Faour, courtesy of Qatar Museums, 2022; 89–91 ©Kyung Roh; 92–95 ©W workspace: Wison Tungthunya; 97–99 ©Maja Wirkus - courtesy of ecoLogicStudio; 101 ©travelpix / Alamy; 103 ©Shane Rounce; 105–107 ©Richter Spielgeräte GmbH; 109 ©Assemble; 113–115 Photos ©Asli Dayioglu for Marmara Forum; 117 ©Iwan Baan; 118 top ©Iwan Baan, bottom ©Torben Eskerod; 119 ©Iwan Baan; 121 ©Wu Qingshan; 123 ©John Lander/ Alamy Stock Photo; 125 ©ZipWorld; 126 ©Andre Pattenden; 129 ©David Levene; 131–133 ©Mark Cocksedge, images courtesy Yinka Ilori Studio; 135–137 ©Amey Kandalgaonkar, images courtesy 100architects; 139–141 ©Lukasz Michalak, courtesy Aberrant Architecture; 143–145 Daniel Buren, Comme un jeu d'enfant, travail in situ, MAMCS, Strasbourg, juin 2014. Détails. ©DB-ADAGP Paris 2024; 147 ©Wanås Konst/ Mattias Givell; 148 ©Conchi Martínez / Alamy; 151–153 ©David Christian Lichtag / GASK; 156 ©Loop Images Ltd / Alamy; 158 top ©Martin Brink / Alamy, bottom ©Ann Waldvogel; 159 ©Guy Bell / Alamy; 160–162 ©Mathery; 164–167 ©Ju Yeon Lee, courtesy of Maum Studio; 168 ©Snøhetta / Patrick Lüth; 170 ©Mark Cocksedge; 171 ©Randall Media / Ashley Wiggins; 172 ©Toshi's Nets ©OliOli® Children's Museum Dubai; 174–177 ©Rex Zou, image courtesy 100architects; 178–181 ©Jonathan Hillyer; 183 image ©Chiara Ye design ©ArkA; 187–189 ©Kostyantyn Skrytutskyy, photography by Misha Kresan; 191 ©Marleen Kuipers; 192 top ©Bouwbedrijf van Middendorp, bottom ©Jelle Draper; 193 ©Mike Bink; 194 ©Ole Barslund Nielsen; 197–199 ©Florentijn Hofman; 201 ©Tim Stet, image courtesy Luca Boscardin Studio; 203–205 ©Seungjae Lee, images courtesy Studio OKGO; 207–209 ©Lewis Allan; 210 ©Earthscape; 212–215 Project by Sulkin Askenazi, Photography ©Aldo C Gracia; 217 ©Sarit Shani Hay; 218–221 ©HEJM Foto; 222 design by by Matter Design & FR|SCH Projects, Image ©Brandon Clifford; 227–229 ©Ketsiree Wongwan; 231 ©Thibault Jeanson, courtesy of Ann Hamilton Studio; 232 ©Isak Heartstone by Thomas Dambo; 235 ©EDU Vision / Alamy; 236 ©Saratstock; 238 ©Paolo Certo; 239 ©Valkantina / Alamy; 241–242 ©Friends of La Laguna 2023; 242 ©Boon Leng Teo; 245 ©Sergio Grazia; 247–249 ©CreatAR Images, images courtesy Wutopia Lab; 251 ©Ole Barslund Nielsen; 253 ©Eddie Gerald / Alamy; 254 ©Ossip van Duivenbode; 256 ©Rasmus Hjortshøj/Coast Studio for JAJA Architects; 259 ©Yihao Hu, courtesy XISUI Design; 261–263 ©SFAP courtesy of X+ Living; 265–267 ©City Museum; 268 ©BASE

Colophon

The Art of Play
First edition, first printing

Published in 2024 by Hoxton Mini Press, London

Text by Emmy Watts
Editing by Zoë Jellicoe
Design by Richard Mason
Proofreading by Florence Ward
Editorial support by Leona Crawford

Thank you to all of the individuals and institutions who have provided images and arranged permissions. While every effort has been made to trace the present copyright holders we apologise in advance for any unintentional omission or error, and would be pleased to insert the appropriate acknowledgement in any subsequent edition.

A CIP catalogue record for this book is available from the British Library.

ISBN: 978-1-914314-69-8

Printed and bound by Livonia Print

Hoxton Mini Press is an environmentally conscious publisher, committed to offsetting our carbon footprint. This book is 100 per cent carbon compensated, with offset purchased from Stand For Trees.

Every time you order from our website, we plant a tree:
www.hoxtonminipress.com

FSC www.fsc.org MIX Paper | Supporting responsible forestry FSC® C002795

Index